Charles Badger Clark was only one of many poets and writers who had a love affair with the Black Hills. Badger Clark—South Dakota's beloved "Poet Lariat"—lived for three decades in his cabin deep inside Custer State Park. In 1927, Badger Clark wrote a friend:

"Half an hour ago I went out on the porch and listened to the eerie chorus of the coyotes across the gulch in the timber... The wind rises outside and I hear it in the tall pines on the hill,...the oldest sound on earth except the sound of falling water; trees of the pine family sang that deep, sonorous song many millenniums before any leaves lisped their little lyrics to the summer breeze. Then, always in the stillest hours, there's the creek—that voice began to murmur before there were any ears on earth to hear it... There's something so resting about these permanencies... It's good, every so often, to get out into the silent places—so silent that you can hear the passing footsteps of God."

***O**ne of Deadwood's imposing main street buildings from the late 19th century. Deadwood's first townsite went up in flames September 26, 1879, as a bakery explosion ignited gunpowder in an adjoining hardware store. Nearly 300 wooden buildings were destroyed.*

A Autumn in the Black Hills is not the only time to visit
Spearfish Canyon, but it is the most spectacular time.
Color is everywhere, and Mother Nature attends the celebration

in her very best party gown. Spruce, pines, golden aspen,
and red willow are but a few varieties of flora seen here
to be captured on film and enjoyed forever.

Bison graze contentedly in the 73,000-acre Custer State Park.

The **Black Hills** are located in southwestern South Dakota and a portion of northeastern Wyoming.
The majority of the land lies within the 1.2-million-acre Black Hills National Forest.

Edited by Cheri C. Madison.
Book design by K. C. DenDooven.

Forth Printing, 2005

Destination - BLACK HILLS: The Story Behind the Scenery.
© 2001 KC PUBLICATIONS, INC.

"The Story Behind the Scenery"; the Eagle / Flag are registered
in the U.S. Patent and Trademark Office.

LC 2001089713. ISBN 0-88714-221-4.

Front cover: Cathedral Spires, Needles Highway,
Custer State Park. Inside front cover: Bison cow and
her newborn calf along Wildlife Loop, Custer State
Park. Page 1: Deadwood Inn, 27 Deadwood Street.
Pages 2/3: Crow Peak, Spearfish Canyon.

BLACK HILLS

THE STORY BEHIND THE SCENERY®

by Beverly Pechan

Beverly Pechan, published writer, researcher, artist, and devotee of Black Hills and frontier history, lives in Keystone, South Dakota, just three miles from Mount Rushmore. She is a founder of the West River History Conference in Keystone and former director of Fort Meade Cavalry Museum near Sturgis.

Photography by Dick Kettlewell

His father's State Department position moved Dick Kettlewell's family to three continents. Fascinated with North American wildlife, Dick began his photojournalism career over 20 years ago after graduating from Chadron State College in Nebraska and a stint in public television work. Dick is a staff photographer at the *Rapid City Journal*.

Your tour starts here, in downtown "cowtown" Rapid City. Dating to 1876, Rapid City began as a hay camp and supply center for freighters, cattle drovers, and stagecoach travelers. It then grew as a hospitality-oriented gateway to the Black Hills' vacationland. Unique to Rapid City is its wide variety of architectural styling and outdoor art. Italianate, Queen Anne, Tudor, and Art Deco designs are represented. The Buell building is from the 1880s and was once a U.S. weather station. Rapid City also boasts an eclectic mix of vintage neon signs.

*"...a line drawn north and south through
Rapid City very nearly divides the hill
from the level or plains region."* —FATHER PETER ROSEN, 1895

Into Black Hills Country

The clanking of harnesses and the shouts of stagecoach drivers broke the calm of the pristine Black Hills as hungry gold seekers, would-be merchants, gamblers, and floozies descended upon the countryside in earnest in 1876. Slowly, families began to trickle into the region, adding some stability to the towns that were springing up everywhere. By the summer of 1875 and into the early part of 1876, the "booming metropolis" known as Custer City was home to dozens and soon thousands of tents and shacks. Then gold was discovered in Deadwood, and settlements emptied overnight in the rush to the new El Dorado. In Hill City, only an elderly man and his dog were left behind to fend for themselves.

Rapid City found its beginnings not in gold diggings, but in supplying the needs of miners, ranchers, and travelers. Hotels began as crude log hovels, soon progressing to two-story frame buildings with eating establishments that also often served as post or telegraph offices. In Rapid City a large stage barn was located in the Gap, at the bottom of what is now known as Dinosaur Park, on the city's west side. Horses were rested and fed here, and it was common to

Canyon Lake City Park is only one of many excellent recreational areas within Rapid City limits and nearby. Playgrounds, picnicking, foot and bike paths, tennis, swimming, and golf are just some of the leisure activities enjoyed in friendly surroundings. With fine museums, entertainment and concert facilities, accommodations and shopping, Rapid City remains at the center of the Black Hills experience.

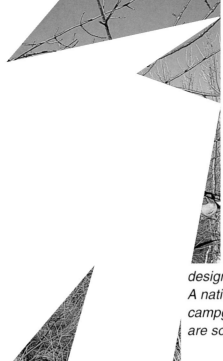
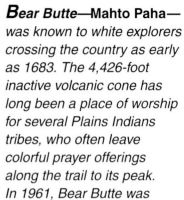

Bear Butte

Bear Butte—Mahto Paha—
was known to white explorers
crossing the country as early
as 1683. The 4,426-foot
inactive volcanic cone has
long been a place of worship
for several Plains Indians
tribes, who often leave
colorful prayer offerings
along the trail to its peak.
In 1961, Bear Butte was
designated as a state park.
A national hiking trail, lake,
campground, and visitor center
are some of today's amenities.

see freighting companies using teams of oxen coming and going from this oasis along Rapid Creek. In 1877, the town's first hanging took place on the hill above the stage barn, when three alleged horse thieves received their fate at the hand of vigilante justice.

Tourism began early around the Black Hills. In 1891, Dr. Valentine McGillycuddy—army surgeon, Indian agent, and Rapid City entrepreneur who was at the time head of the power and light company—proposed to create an electrical sea monster spewing steam, which would rise out of Canyon Lake at intervals and thrill the public beyond belief.

It didn't happen, but in 1917 and 1918, Rapid City built two gigantic Alfalfa Palaces right downtown and had some great celebrations. The buildings, which were torn down shortly after each exposition, were elaborate affairs completely covered with alfalfa and other native grasses. Stockmen's Days, the cattlemen's convention, brought enthusiasts by special trains from Omaha, Chicago, St. Paul, and other points. Lakota Sioux Indians moved their camps to town and participated in the parades, rodeos, races, and sham battle reenactments where the cowboys and the Indians duked it out in playful mayhem.

When it was announced in 1927 that sculptor Gutzon Borglum was going to carve a memorial from a mountain only 20 miles away, Rapid City boosters saw opportunity around every corner. They proposed to hold a Pageant of America by presenting historical tableaus and requiring citi-

zens to dress in authentic costume. When Al Capone was unwelcome in Chicago, he was officially invited to make his home in the Black Hills because he loved to fish and it was thought his celebrity would be a drawing card. The Black Hills was also proposed as the permanent site for the United Nations, and the endeavor came very near to being enacted.

Rapid City has grown gracefully. "The Star of the West," as it is known, is still the hub of Black Hills activity and hospitality. An hour's drive from Rapid City will take you to almost any other attraction in the Hills.

Among Rapid City's many fine museums are The Journey, which traces the history of the region from its earliest beginnings to the present; the natural history museum at the South Dakota School of Mines; the Dahl Fine Arts Center and cyclorama; and children's attractions—like enchanting Storybook Island, a make-believe Mother Goose land near Canyon Lake Park.

Downtown's restored Alex Johnson Hotel remains a local tourist headquarters and retains its 1920s décor of American Indian and Art Deco themes. Rapid City's latest civic beautification project is the placement of life-size bronze statues of American presidents on each street corner.

When Sturgis was laid out in 1878, it was named for Colonel Samuel Sturgis, an officer of the Seventh Cavalry and later commander of nearby Fort Meade. Sturgis, whose brother-in-law was one of the town's founders, also had a financial interest

Fort Meade

Built in 1878 by Custer's reorganized Seventh Cavalry after the Battle of the Little Big Horn, Fort Meade was first commanded by the colorful and unfortunate Major Marcus A. Reno. Comanche, the battle's surviving horse, roamed Fort Meade as post mascot. Soldiers at Fort Meade—named for Civil War general George Gordon Meade, and called "the peacekeeper post"—were instrumental in quelling hostilities and protecting settlers on the new frontier. From 1880 to 1888, the Twenty-fifth Infantry of black soldiers—"buffalo soldiers"—shared duties with the Seventh Cavalry at Fort Meade.

In 1892, commanding officer Col. Caleb Carlton of the Eighth Cavalry, through the suggestion of Mrs. Carlton, ordered Fort Meade's regimental band to play "The Star-Spangled Banner" every evening at retreat and other special observances. Use of this stirring military air was encouraged by Carlton and soon adopted at other installations. In 1931, Congress officially named "The Star-Spangled Banner" America's national anthem.

Located two miles east of Sturgis on SD Highway 34, the Fort Meade museum covers the history of the fort from 1878 to 1944. Fort Meade is also a Veterans Administration medical center, and the Bureau of Land Management (BLM) oversees the old military reservation for historic preservation and public recreational uses.

Fort Meade's post cemetery lies a short distance from faded echoes of bugles, rattling sabers, and thundering hoofs. Resting under sheltering pines is Medal of Honor recipient Albert Knaak, who died on April 7, 1897. Medal of Honor winner Charles Windolph lived to be nearly 100 and is buried at nearby Black Hills National Cemetery.

in the townsite. Bawdy from its beginnings, Sturgis was called "Scooptown," for the way it emptied soldiers' pockets on paydays. Perhaps the town's most successful "merchant" was Poker Alice Tubbs—a faro-dealing, cigar-smoking madam known to almost everyone in the Black Hills, and who was reported to have kept the town solvent.

Major Marcus Reno, first commander at Fort Meade, was ousted by Sturgis, who accused him of window peeping on his lovely daughter, Ella. The story unfolds at the Fort Meade Museum. Visit Poker Alice's home, her gravesite in Sturgis's St. Aloysius Cemetery, the monument to Pony Express rider Charles Nowlin—and check out the infamous Road Kill Café.

Barbecue, sausages, lemonade, and beer are the primary Epicurean fare at the world's biggest motorcycle bash, and if there ever was a people-watching mecca, this is it. Every August, the Hills come alive with rolling thunder as bikers from across America and many nations converge on Sturgis for a week of races, concerts, partying, and carnival atmosphere. Shopping for local T-shirts, leather, and related souvenirs while attending the Sturgis Rally is one of the state's biggest economic boosts. Bikers unanimously say the Black Hills is also their favorite vacation destination.

With his hands full of handlebars, this enterprising rider finds another way to record the action.

Sturgis Rally

Call it a little "backyard get-together" that got out of control, and that pretty much sums up the Sturgis motorcycle rally. In 1938, city ice man and motorcycle enthusiast J. C. "Pappy" Hoel and his wife, Pearl, invited some fellow riders over for a little two-wheeler fun and games and a tour of the Black Hills. Soon they formed a club called "the Jackpine Gypsies," and the party became an annual event. Races were held on a local track, and over the years, the little town of Sturgis welcomed more and more bikers with fewer and fewer places to put them.

By the time the official 50th anniversary of the Sturgis Rally—or Black Hills Motor Classic—or Sturgis Rally and Races, as it is also referred to—rolled around in 1990, the number of fans estimated to be on hand in this town of around 8,000 was from 350,000 to 500,000—or nearly half to three-fourths the entire population of South Dakota! In spite of all its rowdiness, Bike Week in Sturgis has seen relatively few casualties, though today's rally is adult entertainment and not for the shy and inhibited. Whatever can be imagined is likely to be found here in multiples. Still, it's hard to stay away—you never know when you might miss something!

Logos are status symbols for many who come to Sturgis during Bike Week. Custom designs convert motorcycles into airbrushed works of art.

To get a better view, camera towers are set up at both ends of Sturgis's main street. Sidewalk spectators are as thick as motorcycles as they crowd their way past vendors.

SITE OF CAPTURE OF THE ASSASSIN JACK MCCALL WHO SHOT "WILD BILL" HICKOK AUG. 2, 1876

S D HI-WAYS

L VII

Deadwood

Deadwood, one of the West's most rip-roarin' towns, began with a gold strike on February 11, 1876. On August 20 a stagecoach with 20 armed guards headed for Cheyenne, carrying over half a million dollars in gold dust. Other camps emptied overnight in the stampede to this new El Dorado. In October, 300,000 pounds of supplies arrived in Deadwood.

James Butler "Wild Bill" Hickok was a legend before he ever reached Deadwood. His fame made him several enemies, however, and he was gunned down in a card game inside Saloon No. 10 on August 2, 1876. His assassin, Jack McCall, claimed Hickok had killed his brother. McCall was acquitted, but later, bragging of his deed, was recaptured and hung. Wild Bill and his equally notorious acquaintance Calamity Jane are buried side by side in Deadwood's Mount Moriah Cemetery. His hand of aces and eights has since been called "the dead man's hand."

WILD BILL J.B.HICKOCK Killed by the Assasin JACK McCALL ~in~ DEADWOOD BLACK HILLS. August 2nd 1876. Pard We Will meet Again in the happy hunting ground to part no more.

GOOD BYE

Bright lights and jingling jackpots make up downtown Deadwood's character these days. Old-time trolleys creep up and down hilly streets, carrying gamblers from place to place and offering sightseers a relaxed glimpse of the city. Deadwood observes many annual events—like Chinese New Year and Mardi Gras—with colorful street celebrations. Days of '76 in late summer features rodeos, parades, and fun. Car, movie, and music buffs will find plenty to do here, too.

About Deadwood

Deadwood hasn't changed much since 1876. Wild Bill and Calamity never left. Near them in Mount Moriah Cemetery with other Wild West notables is Fred, the parrot companion of notorious Dora DuFran. (Dora's there, too.) Sheriff Seth Bullock, a loyal pal to President Theodore Roosevelt, built a monument to him on top of Mount Roosevelt, just outside of Deadwood. Seth's ghost is said to roam the halls of his famous Bullock Hotel, and the Queen Anne Adam's House, home of Deadwood's wealthiest and most tragic family, is newly restored in Deadwood's Presidential neighborhood. Nearby in Lead, the Homestake, once the largest gold mine on the North American continent, gets ready to take on new life. Tour its open cut and take in both the town's excellent museums. Both Deadwood and Lead are near Terry Peak and Deer Mountain ski areas. On November 1, 1989, exactly a century after statehood, Deadwood once again became South Dakota's gambling hot spot. Its casinos are open 24 hours a day year-round.

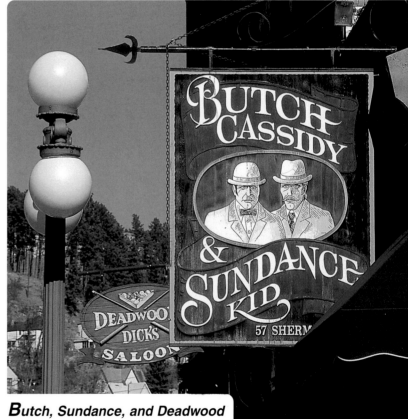

Butch, Sundance, and Deadwood Dick were real folks who knew their way around Deadwood in wilder times. In 1989, Deadwood began restoration of its business district, obtaining designation of the entire area as a National Historic Site. Limited stakes gambling, re-enacted as part of Deadwood's heritage, helped to pay for the renovations.

*The fertile valleys around Spearfish in
the Northern Hills are some of the best
grazing country to be found anywhere.*

Spearfish & Beyond

Spearfish, gateway to Spearfish Canyon, is a modern trade center with a quality of life that is especially attractive to families and retirees. Emerald green golf courses beckon, and the pure mountain air (elevation 3,657 feet) is as good as it gets anywhere. Beginning in 1938, Josef Meier portrayed the Christus in the magnificent Black Hills Passion Play he produced in Spearfish. Members of the Meier family continue the tradition, with a cast of 200 performing in their large amphitheater several nights a week during the summer. Matthews Opera House, a genuine turn-of-the-century opera house turned performing arts center, is in downtown Spearfish. Langer's Black Hills Silver jewelry is fashioned here, and because it's a college town, there's no end to great weekend music for all tastes. At the annual Festival in the Park, large crowds gather to view and buy the best works of today's artists.

The Northern Hills region is the center for winter sports. Over 300 miles

Crow Peak and Spearfish Canyon show off their fall splendor. In this vicinity, the hauntingly beautiful winter scenes from Kevin Costner's Academy Award-winning movie, "Dances with Wolves," were filmed. The area can be easily reached from SD Highway 14A near Savoy.

A popular Northern Black Hills beauty spot, Roughlock Falls was so named because of its rugged terrain and the need for emigrants to "roughlock," or brake, their wagons while trying to navigate dangerously steep passages.

Majestic formations of ancient Pahasapa limestone tower above Spearfish Canyon Scenic Byway. This exhilarating yet gentle 19-mile drive meanders past lofty cliffs and dense forests between Spearfish and Cheyenne Crossing in the Northern Hills on SD Highway 14A. It is a must-see day or weekend trip for photographers and scenery lovers of all ages. Sparkling Spearfish Creek babbles and gurgles as it dances over pebbles and around boulders along the route, inviting you to dip your toes in its refreshing coolness. Disappearing and suddenly reappearing downstream, crystal clear water ripples north, paralleling the highway to join the Belle Fourche River. You'll see Bridal Veil Falls and an assortment of fly fishermen who will usually wave back.

Spearfish

Colorful blooms welcome visitors at the entrance to the "Queen City," Spearfish. A progressive community of over 8,000, Spearfish is home to Black Hills State University, High Plains Heritage Museum, and the Black Hills Passion Play.

BEVERLY PECHAN

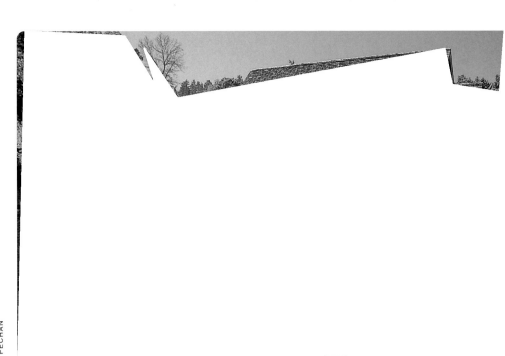

D. C. Booth Historic Fish Hatchery has been an important part of the Spearfish community for nearly a century. The National Fish Culture Hall of Fame and Museum is here, and friendly trout share their ponds with happy, quacking ducks—both hope visitors will feed them. Though trout fishing and eating is a popular Black Hills pastime, trout are not native and were imported in the late 1800s.

of groomed snowmobile trails await you in the O'Neill Pass area between Spearfish and Wyoming's state line. Cross-country and downhill skiing is great here, with the heaviest snowfalls in the Black Hills.

Scenic drives near Spearfish include Icebox Canyon, Vanocker Canyon, and Boulder Canyon at the southern end of Spearfish Canyon on the way back to Rapid City. At Cheyenne Crossing junction, it's time to stop at the little store to gas up and try one of their famous Indian tacos. You're not far from Terry Peak and Deer Mountain ski resorts. Even if it happens to be summer, hop aboard a chair lift for a panoramic view of the countryside.

Ranching, lumbering, and agriculture—as well as mining—have been carried on in and around Spearfish and in the neighboring Whitewood and Centennial districts for over a century. Lush valleys and open prairies between the Bear Butte and Spearfish creeks of South Dakota, and along the Belle Fourche and Redwater rivers extending into Wyoming, were the end of the trail for thousands of Texas and Southwestern beef

herds that began arriving in 1876 and 1877. Here longhorn cattle grew fat, and soon railroad shipping points were established that connected with major markets to the south and east.

Famous cattle empires like the XIT, Matador, Turkey Track, VVV, and Diamond A had operations in and around the Black Hills into the early 20th century. Sheep and horse raising, sugar beets, hay, grain, and garden produce have provided economic diversity in times both good and bad. In Spearfish, High Plains Heritage Museum just off Interstate 90 is devoted to the history of this colorful era, as are the interesting Tri-State Museum in Belle Fourche and the Rockpile Museum in Gillette, Wyoming.

Wyoming's portion of the Black Hills is carved through red rocks and cliffs that are dotted with vegetation on either side of the Bear Lodge Mountains, which rise inside the triangle between Aladdin, Sundance, and Devils Tower. Southwest of Devils Tower following US Highway 14, the Belle Fourche River flows into the Keyhole

Devils Tower National Monument

Reservoir at Keyhole State Park, a popular spot for water sports, north of Moorcroft.

Inyan Kara, a huge basalt mound near Sundance, bears striking similarity to Bear Butte. Custer's name was carved on top of the mountain—a landmark on the Custer expedition to the Black Hills—by a member of his party. Locals, concerned that it would be desecrated by souvenir hunters, have taken pains to conceal the exact location.

And just when you think you've seen it all, there is the curiosity of Devils Tower. Standing alone on the high plains and reaching toward the sky, it is easy to picture in your mind the colorful Indian legend about the Mato, a giant bear that clawed his way to the top of the peak to reach seven

frightened little girls. As the girls tried to flee, it is said the rock rose out of the ground, carrying the girls to the heavens, where they became part of a constellation. Sci-fi movie fans will also recognize this site from "Close Encounters of the Third Kind."

The Red Beds and Tower hiking trails encircle Devils Tower's base for three miles and one and a third miles, respectively. The prairie dog town at the entrance to the monument is sure to take up some of your time, so do allow a few extra minutes in your busy schedule. Climbing the tower is prohibited in certain areas and at various times of the year; park permission is necessary.

The Belle Fourche ("Beautiful Fork") River flows around the northern tip of the Bear Lodge Mountains in Wyoming's portion of the Black Hills National Forest. This is antelope country, and you can expect to see a cowboy or two en route to Devils Tower or Keyhole State Park. Aladdin's general store is a quaint bit of Wyoming history, and the region to the south still has some of the nation's busiest coal mines.

Proclaimed America's first national monument by President Theodore Roosevelt in 1906, Devils Tower challenges the climbing skills of scores who try to reach the top of the 867-foot monolith.

Mountain biking, hiking, and horseback riding are just a stone's throw from Deerfield Lake on well-defined trails. Located northwest of Hill City on Forest Service Road 17, serene and deep blue Deerfield Lake is known as the "ice box" of the Black Hills—hard frosts come early and temperatures can dip quickly.

The Western meadowlark can be heard trilling its cheerful song in open areas throughout the region.

Many species of wildlife call the Black Hills National Forest home. Sure-footed Rocky Mountain goats, like this kid, are adept at climbing slippery, moss-covered slopes. Their large hoofs act as suction cups, helping them to scale near-vertical heights. Bighorn sheep, such as these ewes, are not native to the Black Hills; they were introduced in 1924 to replace Audubon sheep, which became extinct in 1920.

Nature provides ample opportunity to enjoy simple beauty on a rainy afternoon in Black Hills backcountry. The mountain meadows between Rochford and Mystic are profuse with the colors of black-eyed Susans and ox-eye daisies surrounded by timothy grass and forests of Black Hills spruce.

About the Black Hills National Forest

Congress in 1893 provided for the 1.2-million-acre Black Hills Forest Reserve to oversee and protect this vast natural resource. During the gold rush of the two previous decades, countless trees were felled for buildings and massive mine frames, and for fueling huge boilers. The first commercial timber sale from a national forest was called "Case No. 1" and was from the Black Hills to Homestake Mining Company in November 1899. Seth Bullock was forest supervisor. In 1907, the name was changed to the Black Hills National Forest. Public campgrounds, picnic areas, marinas, and 75 hiking and multi-use trails, managed by the U.S. Forest Service, are found throughout the Black Hills—including the 113-mile Mickelson Trail. The 110-mile Centennial Trail and US Highway 385/the Black Hills Parkway, like the Mickelson Trail, run north to south through the length of the Black Hills. More rugged terrain is found within the Norbeck Wildlife Preserve and Black Elk National Wilderness near Mount Rushmore, Custer State Park, and Harney Peak.

Merriam's turkey toms strutting their stuff. Large flocks of wild turkeys are often sighted, being most often seen in the Central Hills and in Custer State Park. This dynamic duo was captured by the photographer just off Pink Cabin Road near Hill City.

Gold mining here was soon followed by tin, copper, and other ventures. Each era had its boom and bust times.

Gold!

Rumors of gold had been breathed about softly at forts and training posts along the frontier for some time. As early as 1855, Ferdinand V. Hayden climbed Bear Butte and declared, "there is gold here." At Fort Laramie, Indians showed off shiny nuggets to missionaries, who encouraged them to keep the secret to themselves. Gold was also said to have been found in paying quantities in the Big Horn country. So it was not surprising that following the national financial panic of 1873, the government decided to send a "mapping detail" into the depths of the Black Hills, where no white man had ventured to go before (at least, none returned to tell of it), and selected two civilian miners to tag along—just in case. Leading the van of 1,200 men, 110 wagons, and a herd of 300 cattle was the indefatigable Lt. Colonel George Armstrong Custer.

While spending two days in a park-like setting east of the town which now bears his name, Custer climbed Harney Peak, while others amused themselves

Hill City is the regional arts center in the Black Hills. Galleries like this artists' co-op flourish by representing talented local artisans and craftsmen. "The Great Quilt Escape"— a real outdoor "hanging"— takes place in September. Look for summer and fall shows and festivals, too.

BEVERLY PECHAN

Old West antics are what one can expect in Hill City. Several nights a week during the summer, the town's businessmen get together and stage a little shootout and other shenanigans along Hill City's historic Main Street.

ROBB DEWALL

Crazy Horse Memorial, largest sculpture in the world, rises 62-1/2 stories (563 feet) into Dakota skies—taller than the Washington Monument. In 1939, noting the progress of nearby Mount Rushmore, Chief Henry Standing Bear of the Lakota Sioux asked sculptor Korczak Ziolkowski (1908-1982) for a mountain carving to show that "the red man has great heroes too." Crazy Horse, revered by his people, was chosen by the Indians. In 1948, Ziolkowski began carving the nonprofit memorial with drills and explosives in the Southern Black Hills. Millions of tons of granite have already been removed as the full dimensional image continues to emerge. Once a year in early June, the country's largest Volksmarch (organized hike) allows hikers to trek to Crazy Horse's outstretched arm for an eagle's-eye view of the Hills. The memorial includes a 40,000-square-foot orientation center and theatre, the Indian Museum of North America, and the Native American Educational and Cultural Center.

Preceding pages: Harney Peak (elevation 7,242 feet) in the Central Hills is the highest U.S. point east of the Rocky Mountains.

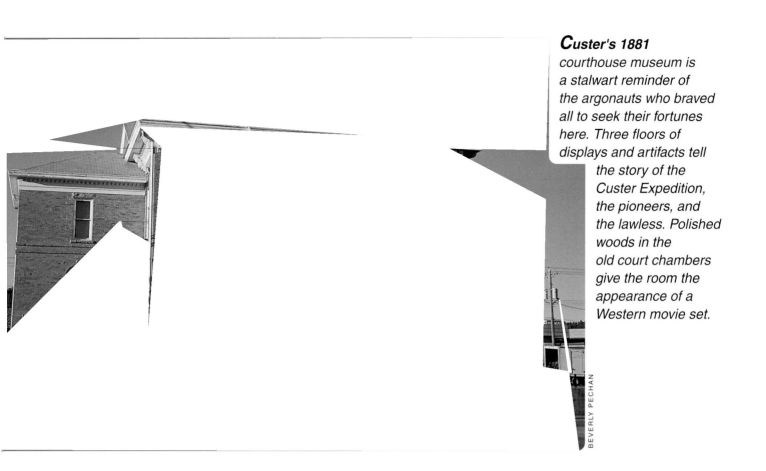

Custer's 1881 courthouse museum is a stalwart reminder of the argonauts who braved all to seek their fortunes here. Three floors of displays and artifacts tell the story of the Custer Expedition, the pioneers, and the lawless. Polished woods in the old court chambers give the room the appearance of a Western movie set.

BEVERLY PECHAN

with a champagne party, concerts, and baseball games. When miner Horatio N. Ross let out a whoop and waved his hat in the air, it proved to be the second "shot heard round the world," as "Lonesome Charley" Reynolds headed toward Fort Laramie with the news.

Within weeks, the Collins-Russell party left Sioux City, Iowa, dodging military patrols and roving bands of Indians, on their way to seek their fortunes. At the eastern edge of the Black Hills, they picked up Custer's trail and followed it south to French Creek. Captain of the group was John Gordon, and history has since referred to this band of emigrants as the Gordon party. In it were 26 men, a woman, Annie Tallent, and her nine-year-old son, Robert.

Arriving in December 1874, they "celebrated" the first Christmas in the Black Hills inside a palisaded log perimeter called the Gordon Stockade. Some did not remain, and the rest were routed by the cavalry the following April. Earlier attempts to reach the group in late December and January were thwarted by "the mercury at forty below zero."

Keeping gold hunters out of the Black Hills was an exercise in futility, however. While it was the army's goal early on to construct a fort as a base of operations to keep intruders out, it soon became evident that a fort would be needed to protect these squatters from Indian attacks and disputes over illegally gotten claims. Thousands were already at the diggings.

Colorful "California Joe" Milner and Ben Ash guided overloaded wagon trains down from Bismarck, following Custer's trail. Dust clouds rolled for miles as plodding ox trains headed for Deadwood with tons of machinery and supplies from the Missouri River landing at Fort Pierre, 200 miles east. Everybody, it seemed, was going to the Black Hills.

Other towns sprang up and died as ores ran out: Gayville, Terraville, Diamond City, Central City, Placerville, Rochford, Mystic, Harney, and more. Sheridan—once a county seat—and Pactola now lie at the bottoms of Sheridan and Pactola lakes, created to provide vital water resources for the region.

In 1880, investors counted on a flume running from Spring Creek at Sheridan to bring much-needed water to Rockerville's placer diggings, to be sold by the miner's inch. The flume, patched daily with rags and horse manure, leaked badly—and in just a few years, Rockerville, too, was in its death throes.

Gold mining was carried on in the Black Hills in boom or bust fashion until World War II, when

Custer

It all started here. On July 30, 1874, Lt. Colonel George Armstrong Custer's Black Hills Expedition camped for two days a mile distant. Ross and McKay, civilian miners with the party, made their way to this site along French Creek to pan for gold and found it. The discovery caused a mad rush to the Black Hills, which was protected by treaty. Within weeks of the announcement, wagon trains were being outfitted in major cities. Many men were attacked and killed en route as the army could not protect them all. Custer City had several thousand inhabitants by the following spring, making it the first permanent settlement in the Black Hills.

BEVERLY PECHAN

the U.S. government closed the gold mines. A renaissance of sorts came along in the 1950s with the local discovery of uranium. In the 1980s, several large operations began mining gold once more in the Northern Hills. The Homestake Mine in Lead was the top-producing gold mine in North America and saw its workers through two world wars, a depression, and other calamities at home and abroad. In 2000, mine officials reluctantly announced that Homestake would be closing after 125 years of continuous operations.

Just as the decade of the 1870s belonged to the argonaut, the fascination with gold in the Black Hills remains strong today. Remnants of old mines dot the Hills, and visitors delight in buying Black Hills Gold jewelry. The story of the jewelry tells of two men en route to the Black Hills who became lost and hungry. One had a fitful dream and awoke to find wild grapes nearby, which sustained them. S. T. Butler, a jeweler, is said to have been the first to create the popular designs in tri-color gold, featuring a classic grape leaf and vein pattern. One of Butler's relatives, F. L. Thorpe, began the first commercial manufacture of Black Hills Gold jewelry in Deadwood in 1879.

***P**anning for gold* is still a favorite pastime for visitors to the Black Hills. Many commercial attractions provide gold pans and instructions, and panning is allowed in some streams on public lands within the Black Hills National Forest. Rocks and minerals of many varieties make great souvenirs; rock shops throughout the Hills carry local specimens in all sizes. Rockhounds will also find the Black Hills a veritable supermarket, but fossil taking is illegal. Rose quartz (pictured here) is found mainly in Custer County and is South Dakota's official mineral. It ranges from pale pink to deep rose and even lavender.

***A** well-worn wagon rests* in the park-like setting where the Custer 1874 expedition camped at the time of the first gold discovery. Custer's men played the first Black Hills game of baseball here in the shadow of Calamity Peak. Still a campground, the historic site is two miles east of Custer City on US Highway 16.

Jewel Cave National Monument

MARC OHMS

What could be better than a room full of diamonds?

How about several rooms full! They aren't real diamonds, of course, and they won't twinkle for you, because these calcite crystals covering the walls and ceilings of Jewel Cave National Monument—which gave the cave its name—are found "in the rough" and are frequently combined with other elements that dull their brilliance in this natural state. In fact, Jewel Cave in the Southern Black Hills contains many treasures. Over 126.5 miles of passageways have been explored so far, making it the second longest cave in the United States and third longest in the world. Beginning in 1959, Herb and Jan Conn of Custer spent 22 years exploring and mapping Jewel Cave from its first mile and a half to over half its located distance. Volunteers, under the direction of National Park Service employees, have taken over where the Conns left off, though no one knows how many miles remain yet undiscovered.

Wind Cave National Park

In 1881, a man riding horseback in the Southern Hills had his hat blown off by a curious gust of wind. Stopping to look around, Tom Bingham noticed a hole near the ground with air rushing through it. In 1890, the McDonald brothers and their father began to examine the cave below and recorded their findings. The McDonalds promoted their oddity, which was given a boost when Theodore Roosevelt gave Wind Cave national park status in 1903. Winds can reach 45 to 70 miles per hour at the entrance when the barometric pressure changes. Wind Cave, located near Hot Springs, is equally known for its lacy boxwork ceilings and other unusual ornamentation, such as flowstone, popcorn, frostwork, and moonmilk. Windy City Lake, a 28-foot-deep subterranean pool inside the cave, is the largest known underground body of water in the Black Hills.

Hot Springs

Hot Springs' 1890s historic district is a registered national landmark recognizing its many fortress-like buildings of locally quarried sandstone. Thousands came annually "to take the waters" and swim in naturally heated Evans Plunge. The Evans Hotel was once a luxury spa with soothing mineral waters piped into every suite.

Natural springs flow year-round near downtown Hot Springs' Fall River Parkway. Locals appreciate the ready availability of this pure water at the Kidney Springs gazebo.

The Hot Springs Area

Long ago, Cheyenne and Lakota Sioux tribes fought on Battle Mountain over claims to the medicinal springs below. The victorious Lakota soon after relinquished them, and moved away. In 1883, Dakota's territorial legislature created Fall River County with over one million acres. Hot Springs later became the county seat. Unlike the rest of the Black Hills, this region is arid and desert-like, supporting yucca and cactus varieties on open grasslands. The oldest sandstone in the Black Hills, the Minnelusa formation, is found here, along with pink Minnekahta limestone. Cretaceous shales and alabaster gypsum lie within the Triassic redbeds that surround Hot Springs. Evans Plunge waters regenerate themselves at 9,000 gallons a minute while maintaining a temperature of 89 degrees. Hot Springs is also the site of a large Veterans Administration complex that includes a Mission-styled sanitarium and retired veterans' homes. Wild horses run free below Cascade Falls off SD Highway 71.

The Mammoth Site south of Hot Springs is one of the few scientific museums in the world that allow the public to watch their work in progress. Experts here are unearthing perhaps 100 skeletal remains of Columbian and woolly mammoths which perished during the late Ice Age. Found in natural positions, they and other species remain trapped in this giant sinkhole from which there was no escape.

> *"Mountains are the beginning and the end of all natural scenery..."* —JOHN RUSKIN, 1819-1900

Custer to Rushmore

From the air, the Black Hills resemble a near-perfect oval called "the racetrack," having the highest points in the center surrounded by thick carpets of forest. Harney Peak is in the center of the Black Hills—a fist of 2.5-billion-year-old Precambrian granite that pushed its way through the earth's crust over 60 million years ago, causing other elements to fall away, creating their own mineral-rich deposits in dikes and ledges. Some sediments crystallized, and in this residue of volcanic magma, much of the region's gold has been found. The Red Valley lies between the Harney granite and limestone deposits and forms the Cretaceous Hogback—rugged Lakota sandstone outcroppings that point the way to 244,000-acre Badlands National Park. The Pierre Sea covered much of the region until about 37 million years ago, continually changing the land's contours and channeling caves below.

Custer State Park was the dream of one man, Senator and Governor Peter Norbeck. Norbeck also envisioned what was later to become Mount Rushmore,

A canoeist paddles close to shore on idyllic Sylvan Lake in Custer State Park's northwestern tip.

Golden sunshine spreads out in secluded profusion along Lower French Creek near Blue Bell Lodge. Giant goldenrods are framed by ponderosa pine forests, which provide cooling shade on a hot summer's day in Custer State Park.

Custer
State
Park

Morning mist rises from Stockade Lake near Custer. Popular with boaters and fishermen, the lake takes its name from neighboring Gordon Stockade, site of the first prospectors' settlement in 1874. Both are located off US Highway 16A inside Custer State Park.

A **Monarch butterfly rests on a leadplant—** also called "the bird's tree" by the Plains Indians, because it is a favorite perch for small songbirds on the open prairie. Butterflies and moths of many species are found throughout the Black Hills.

This pronghorn baby is just hours old and ready for its first meal. Pronghorns are found at lower levels in the Black Hills and on the plains. They are fleet of foot and can reach speeds of about 50 miles per hour. Often called antelope, they are gregarious and will intermingle with cattle in their grazing areas.

"Clowns of the prairie," noisy prairie dogs entertain young and old alike as they cavort and tumble joyously in prairie dog towns. A sharp "yip! yip" warns others when danger approaches, and the population quickly dives into their underground "digs," more commonly called burrows.

JEFF GNASS

The Needle's Eye is only one of Custer State Park's many geological oddities. Rock climbers find parts of its smooth granite surface very difficult to maneuver. Upon reaching the desired destination, an ultimate victory photograph is definitely in order. There are many sites within the park that are available for climbing, and lessons are offered by most outfitters.

and laid out the 66-mile Peter Norbeck Scenic Byway in the Southern Hills, walking the entire area himself, choosing the most scenic routes. One of America's top 10 scenic highways, this system includes the tunnels and pigtail bridges on Iron Mountain Road (US 16A); the Needles Highway (SD 87); Sylvan Lake Road (SD 89); and Horsethief Lake Road (SD 244), leading past Mount Rushmore.

Inside Custer State Park, the Peter Norbeck Visitor Center holds mementos and the history of Norbeck's vision. The adjacent State Game Lodge became the summer White House for President and Mrs. Calvin Coolidge in 1927 and the Dwight D. Eisenhowers in 1953.

Deeper inside Custer State Park, the Black Hills Playhouse has nightly performances throughout the summer. Housed in old Civilian Conservation Corps buildings, it is hard to realize, while relaxing in the rustic log pavilion with your picnic supper, that you are about to see a stellar performance with Broadway professionalism just a few steps away in the "no-traffic middle of nowhere."

George Washington's head is 60 feet tall. Each eye contains a granite "sliver" left in place as a highlight to give the sculpture life. Washington's head was the first carving to be completed on Mount Rushmore and was dedicated with sculptor Gutzon Borglum's usual zeal. The painstaking process of shaping this national memorial can be seen by studying the numerous grids on the left.

Mount Rushmore National Memorial

Mount Rushmore's new 2,000-seat amphitheater and multi-level parking area are only a part of the recent renovation at the memorial. The state-of-the-art Lincoln Borglum Museum contains 5,200 square feet of exhibit space, a bookstore, and two theatres. An exciting new Presidential Trail and boardwalk leads directly underneath "the faces." You may even meet a Rocky Mountain goat along the pathway. Over 2.7 million people a year come to see Mount Rushmore, and whether it is their first time or fiftieth, most say seeing America's "shrine of democracy" is a truly awesome experience.

You will also want to visit "the Badger Hole" while you are in the park. Actually, there are two of them. South Dakota's first poet laureate Charles Badger Clark (he preferred to say "poet lariat") built his first cabin here in 1927 and the second in 1937. They are open to the public and remain as they were at the time of his death in 1957.

The park's Wildlife Loop has everything from noble bison to begging burros. Major fall events are the annual buffalo (bison) roundup and auction, with the proceeds assisting the park's overall budget. South Dakota Highway 79—"The Heartland Express"—parallels Custer State Park to the east and will get you there in no time.

One of the best bargains ever, Mount Rushmore National Memorial took 14 years to cre-ate, at a total cost of less than a million dollars. It was the first time an undertaking of such large proportions was attempted, and many thought it could not be done. Through periods of the Great Depression, sculptor Gutzon Borglum had no funding and no way to pay his men. Donations of schoolchildren added pennies to the coffers—it wasn't enough, of course, but their gestures of good will rekindled the flow of money to keep the project going.

Energetic Borglum was 62 years old when he began work on Mount Rushmore in 1927; Borglum's son, Lincoln, worked at his father's side, ending the work in October 1941, eight months after his father's death. Today, Mount Rushmore is one of America's most patriotic sights.

BEVERLY PECHAN

Anytime is a great time to visit the Black Hills. Horsethief Lake, located near Mount Rushmore and Keystone, is only one of many recreational and trailhead areas close by. Winters in the Central Hills are often mild, with sudden warm-ups. The off, or "shoulder," seasons are becoming attractive to those who prefer less traffic and more leisurely pursuits. Many areas have great snowmobiling and skiing, and most major attractions and visitor centers remain open all year.

Keystone is the home of two distinct mining districts: the upper portion made up of gold mines, and the lower half of tin and pegmatite ores—like the Peerless mica mine and its ore bin, pictured here. Through the 1950s, ores from Keystone mines were shipped all over the world. Some quartz milling and production continues today for industrial uses. Children often find ruby red garnets in Battle Creek, which runs through Keystone.

Brothers Peter and Neal Larson of the Black Hills Institute of Geological Research appear with Tyrannosaurus rex *Stan*, permanent greeter at their Hill City facility and natural history museum. The institute has located and curated important fossils and related specimens for some of the world's most prestigious scientific institutions, including the Smithsonian. Dinosaur fans sometimes can view the restoration work and chat with the Larsons about their mutual favorite subjects.

RICK W. MILLS

All aboard! Railroads have always been an important part of Black Hills history. The Black Hills Central Railroad, also known as the 1880 Train, runs between Hill City and Keystone on original tracks several times a day throughout the tourist season, and is a pleasurable 20-mile round trip through pine-studded backcountry. Expect to see old mining camps, beaver dams, a movie location, and frequently, stops for cud-chewing cattle standing on the railroad ties. The weekend Christmas train is a frosty plus.

Rockerville

BEVERLY PECHAN

Collectors will find the Black Hills a real treat as they browse the many antique emporiums located in nearly every town. Several shops combine enjoyable shopping with nostalgic dining, penny candy counters, and ice cream parlors for a genuine trip back to yesteryear. Whatever you've been searching for, you are likely to find it here.

Not much is left of original Rockerville, but this replica gold camp shows what life was like there in 1880 when miners worked the 17-mile flume and gamblers conducted business at saloon tables. Newspaperman Ambrose Bierce came to Rockerville attempting—unsuccessfully—to straighten out the mining company's affairs. One of his acts was to hire gunman Boone May to guard gold shipments. May was listed on the payroll as "murderer."

BEVERLY PECHAN

It's been a dream of young boys and old men and ages in between to land lunker trout.

Tiny Mitchell Lake on US highways 16 and 385 northeast of Hill City will allow you to do just that from its shores. They're thi-i-i-s big. Honest.

Deer are gracious inhabitants of the Black Hills and its neighboring grasslands. Mule deer and white-tailed deer—like this young buck in velvet—can be found here. "Muleys" are distinguished by their larger size, mousy gray color, and extra-large ears—and, unlike other species, are inquisitive and impulsively curious about humans.

SUGGESTED READING

FROILAND, SVEN. *Natural History of the Black Hills and Badlands.* Sioux Falls, South Dakota: The Center for Western Studies, 1990 (revised ed.).

GREIS, JOHN PAUL. *Roadside Geology of South Dakota.* Missoula, Montana: Mountain Press, 1996.

LEE, BOB. *Fort Meade & The Black Hills.* Lincoln, Nebraska: University of Nebraska Press, 1994.

REZATTO, HELEN. *Tales of the Black Hills.* Aberdeen, South Dakota: North Plains Press, 1984.

JACKSON, DONALD. *Custer's Gold.* Lincoln, Nebraska: University of Nebraska Press, 1966.

STRAIN, DAVID. *Black Hills Hay Camp: Images and Perspectives of Early Rapid City.* Rapid City, South Dakota: Dakota West Books, 1986.

CONN, HERB and JAN. *The Jewel Cave Adventure.* Teaneck, New Jersey: Zephyrus Press, 1977.

FEIFFER, STEVE. *Tyrannosaurus Sue.* New York, New York: W. H. Freeman Co, 2000.

DEWALL, ROBB. *Crazy Horse and Korczak.* Crazy Horse, South Dakota: Korczak's Heritage, Inc., 1983.

SMITH, REX ALLEN. *The Carving of Mount Rushmore.* New York, New York: Abbeville Press, 1985.

SMITH, REX ALLEN. *Moon of Popping Trees.* Lincoln, Nebraska: University of Nebraska Press, 1981.

TOMOVICK and METZ. *Insider's Guide to the Black Hills and Badlands of South Dakota.* Helena, Montana: Falcon Press, 2000.

FROM KC PUBLICATIONS, LAS VEGAS, NEVADA

Badlands: The Story Behind the Scenery, 1997.
Devils Tower: The Story Behind the Scenery, 1991.
Jewel Cave: The Story Behind the Scenery, 1998.
Mount Rushmore: The Story Behind the Scenery, 1993.
Pony Express: Voyage of Discovery, 1999.
Wind Cave: The Story Behind the Scenery, 1998.

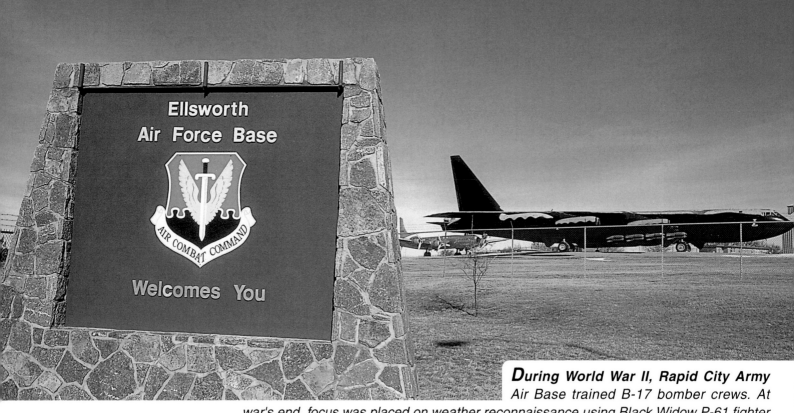

During World War II, Rapid City Army Air Base trained B-17 bomber crews. At war's end, focus was placed on weather reconnaissance using Black Widow P-61 fighter planes. Briefly called Weaver Air Force Base, several name changes occurred before designation as the permanent home of the 28th Bombardment Wing. In 1953, the name was changed again to honor war hero Brigadier General Richard E. Ellsworth. Ellsworth's widow wed Lincoln Borglum, son of Mount Rushmore's sculptor. Ellsworth Air Force Base became an integral part of the Strategic Air Command and the Minuteman Missile program and today is home base for the B-1 bomber. Ellsworth hosts an annual air show, and there is an impressive air and space museum on the grounds.

JOHN P. GEORGE

Though only separated by 50 miles, South Dakota's Badlands National Park bears no resemblance at all to the Black Hills. Frank Lloyd Wright said in 1935, "I was totally unprepared for that revelation called the Dakota Bad Lands." Barren-looking lunarscapes give way to tablelands and basins teeming with wildlife and rich grasses, while sudden storms produce lightning shows unequalled anywhere. The Badlands has an ever-changing beauty all its own.

***"A**ll wired up"* with Christmas lights, the big bronto at Dinosaur
*Park on Rapid City's Skyline Drive stands as a sentinel overlooking
the city. Often seen silhouetted against the sunset, he and his later version concrete cronies bring
your Black Hills tour full circle. Summer, winter, spring, or fall, there is much to see and
do here in the Black Hills of South Dakota and Wyoming. Perhaps nowhere else on the North
American continent will you find so many one-of-a-kind adventures.
Any way you look at it, the view is great.*

Truly, the Black Hills is a paradise. This relatively small area contains five national parks and monuments, three state parks, two memorial mountain carvings, five recreational reservoirs, a national forest and two wilderness preserves, a national grassland, three national scenic byways, a national cemetery, two national and one state fish hatcheries, a wild horse sanctuary with ancient petroglyphs, and nine major caves that offer a variety of tours.

Something spiritually awesome emerges from this beauty. Many say that in the solitude of the Black Hills forests, strength and wisdom come to them. Indians feared the Black Hills' thunder and lightning; artists and writers are inspired by it. Some groups find the Black Hills a mecca for metaphysical pursuits. Here rocks glow in eerie lights and the nights resound with unexplained voices—phenomena observed from earliest times by both the red and the white man.

Sculptor Gutzon Borglum created his patriotic memorial of stone in the pristine wilderness of the Black Hills National Forest as a tribute honoring all Americans "...until the wind and rain alone shall wear them away."

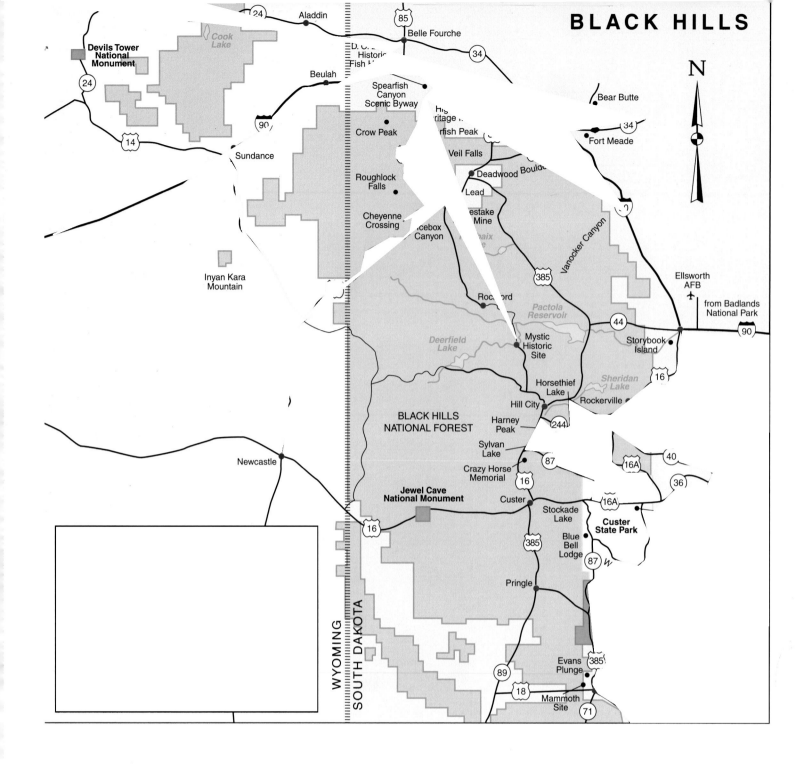

BLACK HILLS

N

Devils Tower National Monument

24

14

Cook Lake

Aladdin

85 Belle Fourche

34

D. C. ... Historic Fish ...

Beulah

Spearfish Canyon Scenic Byway

High ... Heritage ...

...rfish Peak

Bear Butte

34

Fort Meade

90

Crow Peak

Veil Falls

Sundance

Roughlock Falls

Deadwood

Boulder

Lead

...estake Mine

Vanocker Canyon

Ellsworth AFB

from Badlands National Park

90

Cheyenne Crossing

Icebox Canyon

...naix ...e

385

Pactola Reservoir

44

Storybook Island

Inyan Kara Mountain

Roc...ord

Deerfield Lake

Mystic Historic Site

Sheridan Lake

16

Horsethief Lake

Rockerville

Newcastle

BLACK HILLS NATIONAL FOREST

Hill City

Harney Peak

244

Sylvan Lake

87

16A

40

Crazy Horse Memorial

16

36

Jewel Cave National Monument

Custer

16A

WYOMING

SOUTH DAKOTA

16

Stockade Lake

Custer State Park

385

Blue Bell Lodge

87

Pringle

Evans Plunge

385

89

18

Mammoth Site

71

KC Publications has been the leading publisher of colorful, interpretive books about National Park areas, public lands, Indian lands, and related subjects for over 40 years. We have 6 active series—over 135 titles—with Translation Packages in up to 8 languages for over half the areas we cover. Write, call, or visit our web site for our full-color catalog.

Our series are:

The Story Behind the Scenery® – Compelling stories of over 65 National Park areas and similar Public Land areas. Some with Translation Packages.

in pictures... The Continuing Story® – A companion, pictorially oriented, series on America's National Parks. All titles have Translation Packages.

For Young Adventurers™ – Dedicated to young seekers and keepers of all things wild and sacred. Explore America's Heritage from A to Z.

Voyage of Discovery® – Exploration of the expansion of the western United States.

Indian Culture and the Southwest – All about Native Americans, past and present.

Calendars – For National Parks in dramatic full color, and a companion Color Your Own series, with crayons.

To receive our full-color catalog featuring over 135 titles—Books, Calendars, Screen Scenes, Videos, Audio Tapes, and other related specialty products:

Call (800-626-9673), fax (702-433-3420), write to the address below, Or visit our web site at www.kcpublications.com

Published by KC Publications, 3245 E. Patrick Ln., Suite A, Las Vegas, NV 89120.

Inside back cover:
Lakota legends describe the "Moon of the Big Red Calf."

Back cover:
Worker Bob Crisman inspects the Rushmore carvings for cracks.

Created, Designed, and Published in the U.S.A.
Printed by Tien Wah Press (Pte.) Ltd, Singapore
Pre-Press by United Graphic Pte. Ltd